ANIMAL FAMILIES

LIONS
LIFE IN THE PRIDE

Willow Clark

PowerKiDS
press.

New York

Published in 2011 by The Rosen Publishing Group, Inc.
29 East 21st Street, New York, NY 10010

First Edition

Editor: Jennifer Way
Book Design: Julio Gil

Photo Credits: Cover, pp. 9, 24 (top left) Digital Vision/Thinkstock; back cover © www.iStockphoto.com/ vectorcartoons; pp. 4–5, 21, 23, 24 (bottom right) Anup Shah/Photodisc/Thinkstock; pp. 7 (main), 11, 15, 17 (inset top, inset bottom), 24 (top middle, bottom left) iStockphoto/Thinkstock; p. 7 (inset) Hemera/ Thinkstock; p. 12–13 Tom Brakefield/Stockbyte/Thinkstock; p. 16–17 (main) Stockbyte/Thinkstock; p. 19 Anup Shah/Digital Vision/Thinkstock; p. 24 (top right) Jupiterimages/Photos.com/Thinkstock.

Library of Congress Cataloging-in-Publication Data
Clark, Willow.
  Lions : life in the pride / by Willow Clark. — 1st ed.
      p. cm. — (Animal families)
  Includes index.
  ISBN 978-1-4488-2513-4 (library binding) — ISBN 978-1-4488-2612-4 (pbk.) —
  ISBN 978-1-4488-2613-1 (6-pack)
  1. Lion—Juvenile literature. 2. Familial behavior in animals—Juvenile literature. I. Title.
  QL737.C23C5324 2011
  599.757—dc22
                                                2010019303

Manufactured in the United States of America

CPSIA Compliance Information: Batch #WW11PK: For Further Information contact Rosen Publishing, New York, New York at 1-800-237-9932

CONTENTS

Lions live together in a group, called a **pride**.

Lions live in **grasslands** in Africa.

Africa

The pride raises its young together. Young lions are called **cubs**.

Male lions have **manes**. They also roar loudly.

Mane

Female lions are lionesses. Mothers, daughters, and sisters belong to the same pride.

Female cubs stay with their prides. Male cubs join new groups of lionesses.

Lionesses do most of the hunting for the pride. They hunt zebras and wildebeests.

Zebra

Wildebeest

The male lions watch the cubs while the lionesses hunt for the pride's food.

The lionesses bring food back to the pride. The males eat first. The cubs eat last.

Lions rest most of the day. While resting, they sleep, play, and **groom** each other.

Words to Know

cubs

grasslands

groom

mane

pride

Index

Web Sites

Due to the changing nature of Internet links, PowerKids Press has developed an online list of Web sites related to the subject of this book. This site is updated regularly. Please use this link to access the list:
www.powerkidslinks.com/afam/lions/